CW00362789

A COOK'S JOURNAL

The Artist's Kitchen in Francis Street, 1846, George Scharf the
Elder. Department of Prints and Drawings, P&D 1862-6-14-80

THE BRITISH MUSEUM

A COOK'S

JOURNAL

Contents

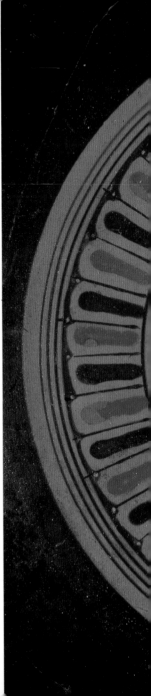

Opposite: A black-figured cup showing a successful huntsman with two hares, *c.* 550 BC. At Athens, hare was the typical game animal. *Above*: A plate depicting Persephone serving Pluto, *c.* 430 BC. Department of Greek and Roman Antiquities, G&R B421 & E82

Starters & Light Dishes

If you sit with a greedy person, eat only when his meal is over, and if you sit with a wine drunkard, take only when his desire is satisfied.

Extract from an Ancient Egyptian text,
c. 2350 BC, entitled the *Instruction of Ka-Gem-Ni.*

Detail from the wooden coffin of Amenemipet, *c.* 950–900 BC, from Thebes, Egypt. Department of Ancient Egypt and Sudan, EA 22941

Fish Dishes

A casserole — no, bigger than that — call it a marmite, full of
noble eel with a look of the conger about him,
Honey-glazed shrimps besides, my love,
Squid sprinkled with sea-salt
Baby birds in flaky pastry,
And a baked tuna, gods! What a huge one, fresh from the
fire and the pan and the carving-knife,
Enough steaks from its tender belly to delight us both as
long as we might care to stay and munch.

The *Banquet* of Philoxenus, *c.* 400 BC, from Sicily or
Greece.

The author of this passage has not, as yet, been
established. Some suppose it was Philoxenus of Leucas –
a well-known glutton – while others imagine it to be
the work of Philoxenus of Cythera, a court poet.

A mosaic floor panel showing edible fish. Thought to be from
Populonia, near Rome, *c.* AD 100. Department of Greek and
Roman Antiquities, GR 1989.3-22.1

Main & Substantial Dishes

In Medieval Europe the upper classes indulged in elaborate feasting. The guests would carry their own knife and spoon around with them because forks were not yet used. At the end of each course, servants would appear with napkins and bowls of water for the guests to clean their hands. It was also customary to eat seeds such as coriander and fennel at the end of a meal in order to sweeten the breath. These seeds were coated one by one in sugar, often taking several days to prepare.

One of seven panels from a Limoges enamel casket, *c.* 1600. This panel shows the feast of Be'rsheba. Department of Medieval and Modern Europe, Waddedson 51

_____

_____

_____

_____

_____

_____

_____

_____

_____

_____

_____

_____

_____

_____

_____

_____

_____

_____

_____

_____

_____

_____

_____

_____

_____

_____

_____

_____

Desserts

At last we had our fill of food and drink:
*   The servants cleared away, and brought warm water, soap and*
oil of orris to wash our hands.
*   They gave us muslin towels, divine perfumes, wreaths of*
*   violets.*
*   Then the same polished tables, loaded up with more good*
things, sailed back to us, second tables as men say:
Sweet pastry shells,
Crispy flapjacks,
Toasted sesame cakes drenched in honey and sauce,
Cheesecake, made with milk and honey, a sweet that was
baked like a pie;
Cheese-and-sesame sweetmeats fried in hottest oil
and rolled in sesame seeds were passed around…

The *Banquet* of Philoxenus, *c.* 400 BC, from Sicily or
Greece.

Details of fruit by Jacques Le Moyne (*c.* 1533–88): Orange,
apple, lemon and pomegranate. Department of Prints and
Drawings, P&D 1962-7-14-1(44), 1962-7-14-1(40), 1962-
7-14-1(42), 1962-7-14-1(45)

Sauces

Gravy and Glaze

'Take a fore Shin of Beef, cut it in pieces, & lay it in a stew
pan with six large onions – Turnip Carrot & two heads of
Cellery, 7 sweet herbs – set it on a stove & draw out the
Gravy, let it be brown & all dried up, then put water to it,
skim it very well & let it boil till very good Gravy – then
strain it through a sieve & when it is cold take off all the
fat, & take any quantity you want, set it on the side of the
stove without a Cover, & let it boil till it is like glue – put
it on anything you wish to Glaze with a paste brush.'

Notebook of Recipes, Martha Lloyd (1765–1843).

Detail from *Cobler's Hall*, late eighteenth century. Engraving,
published by Bowles and Carver, England. Department of
Prints and Drawings, P&D 1875-8-14-2465

Duke of Cumberland

	Stocks, soups and savoury sauces	Vegetable dishes	Savoury grains and pasta	Pulses and beans	Eggs and dairy	Fish	Meat	Poultry and game	Sweet dishes and puddings	Cakes and jams	Pickles, chutneys, preserves, vinegars	Sweet and savoury drinks
Allspice	♦	♦				♦	♦	♦			♦	♦
Angelica									♦	♦		
Aniseed		♦					♦	♦	♦	♦		♦
Basil	♦	♦	♦	♦	♦	♦	♦	♦	♦			
Balm		♦	♦	♦		♦	♦	♦				
Bay	♦	♦	♦	♦	♦	♦	♦	♦				
Bergamot					♦							♦
Borage	♦	♦	♦			♦			♦	♦	♦	♦
Caraway seed	♦	♦	♦	♦			♦			♦		♦
Cardamom	♦	♦	♦	♦	♦		♦	♦			♦	
Cayenne	♦	♦	♦	♦	♦	♦	♦	♦			♦	
Celery seed	♦	♦	♦	♦	♦	♦	♦	♦				♦
Chervil	♦	♦	♦	♦	♦	♦	♦	♦				
Chilli	♦	♦	♦	♦	♦	♦	♦	♦			♦	
Chives	♦	♦	♦	♦	♦	♦	♦	♦				
Cinnamon								♦	♦	♦	♦	♦
Cloves	♦										♦	
Coriander seed	♦	♦	♦	♦	♦		♦		♦	♦	♦	
Coriander leaf	♦	♦	♦	♦	♦	♦	♦	♦				
Cumin	♦	♦		♦	♦	♦	♦				♦	
Curry powder	♦	♦	♦	♦	♦		♦	♦			♦	
Dill	♦	♦	♦	♦	♦	♦		♦			♦	♦
Fennel	♦	♦		♦	♦	♦	♦	♦			♦	
Fenugreek		♦	♦	♦	♦		♦	♦			♦	
Garlic	♦	♦	♦	♦	♦	♦	♦	♦			♦	
Ginger powder	♦						♦	♦	♦	♦	♦	♦
Horseradish						♦	♦	♦			♦	

Stocks, soups and savoury sauces	Vegetable dishes	Savoury grains and pasta	Pulses and beans	Eggs and dairy	Fish	Meat	Poultry and game	Sweet dishes and puddings	Cakes and jams	Pickles, chutneys, preserves, vinegars	Sweet and savoury drinks	
◆	◆				◆	◆	◆			◆	◆	Juniper
◆	◆		◆		◆	◆	◆	◆		◆		Lemon grass
◆	◆	◆	◆	◆	◆	◆	◆			◆	◆	Lovage
◆			◆	◆	◆	◆	◆	◆		◆		Mace
◆	◆	◆	◆	◆	◆	◆	◆			◆	◆	Marjoram
◆	◆	◆	◆	◆	◆	◆	◆	◆		◆	◆	Mint
◆	◆	◆	◆	◆	◆	◆	◆			◆		Mustard
◆	◆	◆	◆	◆	◆	◆	◆	◆	◆	◆	◆	Nutmeg
◆	◆	◆	◆	◆	◆	◆	◆			◆	◆	Oregano
◆	◆	◆	◆	◆	◆	◆	◆			◆	◆	Paprika
◆	◆	◆	◆	◆	◆	◆	◆			◆	◆	Parsley
◆	◆	◆	◆	◆	◆	◆	◆			◆	◆	Peppercorns
								◆	◆			Poppy seed
◆	◆	◆	◆	◆	◆	◆	◆				◆	Rosemary
◆	◆	◆	◆	◆	◆	◆	◆	◆	◆	◆	◆	Saffron
◆	◆	◆	◆	◆		◆	◆			◆	◆	Sage
◆	◆	◆	◆	◆	◆	◆	◆					Savory
◆		◆	◆	◆	◆	◆	◆					Sorrel
◆	◆	◆	◆		◆	◆	◆			◆		Shallots
						◆				◆		Star anise
◆	◆					◆			◆		◆	Sweet cicely
◆	◆				◆	◆	◆			◆	◆	Tamarind
◆	◆				◆			◆			◆	Tansy
◆	◆	◆	◆	◆	◆	◆	◆			◆	◆	Tarragon
◆	◆	◆	◆	◆	◆	◆	◆				◆	Thyme
◆	◆	◆	◆	◆	◆	◆	◆				◆	Thyme, lemon
◆	◆	◆	◆		◆	◆	◆			◆		Turmeric

Wine Cellar

Wine is the best gift of gods to men, sparkling wine; every song, every dance, every passionate love, goes with wine. It drives all sorrows from men's hearts when drunk in due measure, but when taken immoderately it is a bane.

Athenaeus of Naucrates, second century AD.

Athenaeus was reputedly a social commentator from Egypt, who amassed thousands of quotations on the subject of food and wine.

Tile designed by the artist and novelist William De Morgan, (1839–1917). Department of Medieval and Modern Europe, M&ME 1980, 3-7. 6

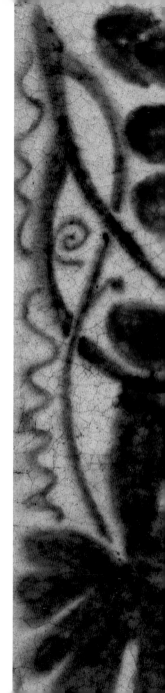

WINE	YEAR & REGION	COMMENTS

WINE	YEAR & REGION	COMMENTS

WINE	YEAR & REGION	COMMENTS

WINE	YEAR & REGION	COMMENTS

IMPERIAL – METRIC/AMERICAN CONVERSIONS
DRY WEIGHTS

Imperial	Metric approx. equivalent	Metric exact equivalent
1/4oz	5g	7.0g
1/2oz	10g	14.1g
1oz	25g	28.3g
2oz	50g	56.6g
3oz	75g	84.9g
4oz	110g	113.2g
8oz	225g	227.0g
12oz	340g	340.0g
16oz (1lb)	450g	454.0g
2lb	900g	898.0g
2 1/4lb	1kg	1.02kg

LIQUIDS

Imperial	Metric approx. equivalent	American equivalent
1/4 pt/5 fl. oz	150ml	2/3 cup
1/2 pt/10 fl. oz	300ml	1 1/4 cups
3/4 pt/15 fl. oz	450ml	2 1/2 cups
1pt/20 fl. oz	600ml	2 cups
1 1/2 pt/30 fl. oz	900ml	3 3/4 cups
1 3/4 pt/35 fl. oz	1 litre	4 cups
2pt/40 fl. oz	1.2 litres	5 cups

IMPERIAL – AMERICAN CONVERSION
DRY WEIGHTS

Imperial	American
8oz fat	1 cup
4oz flour	1 cup
8oz sugar	1 cup
4 1/2oz icing sugar (confectioner's)	1 cup
12oz syrup or treacle (molasses)	1 cup
7oz rice and grains	1 cup
5oz dried fruit	1 cup
2oz fresh breadcrumbs	1 cup
4oz chopped nuts	1 cup

OVEN TEMPERATURES

Dishes	°C	°F	Gas	Temperature
Meringues, drying bread	100	225	¼	Very cool
Bottling fruit	130	250	½	Very cool
Egg dishes and custards, milk puddings, baked fish	140	275	1	Cool
Stews, rich fruit cakes, baked fruit	150	300	2	Slow
Casseroles, slow roasting, braised meat and vegetables, plain fruit cakes	170	325	3	Moderately slow
Madeira cake, Victoria sponge	180	350	4	Moderate
Biscuits, whisked sponges	190	375	5	Moderately hot
Shortcrust pastry, tarts	200	400	6	Hot
Fast roasting, scones, bread, choux pastry	220	425	7	Very hot
Soufflés, puff and flaky pastry, pilaffs, roast potatoes, yeast buns, rolls	230	450	8	Very hot

ROASTING TIMES

Meat	Per 450g	Extra time	Temperature
Lamb	20 mins	+ 20 mins	450–475°F: pink
Beef	15 mins	+ 15 mins	450–475°F: rare
Pork	25 mins	+ 25 mins	450–475°F: well done
Veal	25 mins	+ 25 mins	450–475°F: well done
Bacon	20 mins	+ 20 mins	350°F: 20 mins before end raise to 375°F
Chicken	20 mins	+ 20 mins	375°F
Turkey	20 mins	+ 20 mins	375°F
Duck	30–35 mins	+ 20 mins	375°F
Goose	15 mins	+ 5 mins	375°F
Venison	30 mins	+ 30 mins	start at 450°F, after 10 mins reduce to 375°F

Game bird	Total time
Guinea fowl	45–60 mins
Pheasant	40–50 mins
Grouse	20–30 mins
Partridge	20–25 mins
Woodcock	20–30 mins
Snipe	10–12 mins

Note: when roasting game birds, start at 450°F and after 10 mins reduce to 400°F

NAME	ADDRESS	PHONE

Fragment of painted plaster wall decoration, *c.* 1350 BC. From the tomb of Nebamun, Thebes, Egypt. Department of Ancient Egypt and Sudan, EA 37986

NAME	ADDRESS	PHONE

NAME	ADDRESS	PHONE

NAME	ADDRESS	PHONE

Celebrations

A fragment from the Vindolanda tablets, dated around AD 100. The tablet is a birthday invitation from Claudia Severa to Lepidina, wife of commander Ceralis. It reads: '*Sister, when I celebrate my birthday, I invite you warmly to come to us: you will make the day more enjoyable for me if you are here.*' Department of Prehistory and Early Europe, P 1986-10-1-64

The British Museum Cookbook, Michelle Berriedale-Johnson,
The British Museum Press, paperback edn 1995,
0 7141 1759 5

The Classical Cookbook, Andrew Dalby and Sally Grainger,
The British Museum Press, paperback edn 2000,
0 7141 2222 X

Dangerous Tastes, The Story of Spices, Andrew Dalby,
The British Museum Press, paperback edn 2002,
0 7141 2771 X

Food Fit for Pharaohs, An Ancient Egyptian Cookbook,
Michelle Berriedale-Johnson, The British Museum Press, 1999,
0 7141 1929 6

The Jane Austen Cookbook, Maggie Black and Deirdre Le Faye,
The British Museum Press, paperback edn 2002,
0 7141 2769 8

The Medieval Cookbook, Maggie Black,
The British Museum Press, paperback edn 1996,
0 7141 0583 X

© 2003 The Trustees of the British Museum
First published in 2003 by The British Museum Press
A division of The British Museum Company Ltd
46 Bloomsbury Street, London, WC1B 3QQ

www.britishmuseum.co.uk

ISBN 0 7141 9102 7

Designed by Sara Mathews
Typeset in Bembo
Printed in Hong Kong by H&Y Printing Ltd